D1549051

Say Bonjour to the Lady

PARENTING FROM PARIS TO NEW YORK

Florence Mars & Pauline Lévêque

CLARKSON POTTER/PUBLISHERS

NEW YORK

For Louis, Alice, and Blanche

FLORENCE

For Georges and Clea

PAULINE

Published in the United States by Clarkson Potter/Publishers, an imprint of the Crown Publishing Group,
a division of Penguin Random House LLC, New York.
crownpublishing.com
clarksonpotter.com

CLARKSON POTTER is a trademark and POTTER with colophon is a registered trademark of Penguin Random House LLC.

Library of Congress Cataloging-in-Publication Data
Names: Mars, Florence, author. | Lévêque, Pauline, author.
Title: Say bonjour to the lady : parenting from Paris to New York
Florence Mars and Pauline Lévêque.
Description: First edition. | New York : Clarkson Potter, [2017]
Identifiers: LCCN 2016013222 (print) | LCCN 2016020773 (ebook) | ISBN
9780451495013 (hardcover) | ISBN 9780451495020 (ebook)
Subjects: LCSH: Parents—France—Paris. | Parents—United States. |
Parenting—Humor. | Parenting—Cross-cultural studies.
Classification: LCC HQ755.8 .M357296 2017 (print) | LCC HQ755.8 (ebook) | DDC
306.8740944/361—dc23
LC record available at https://lccn.loc.gov/2016013222

ISBN 978-0-451-49501-3
eBook ISBN 978-0-451-49502-0
Printed in China

Book design by Debbie Glasserman
Cover design by Debbie Glasserman

10 9 8 7 6 5 4 3 2 1
First Edition

Contents

Iwas raised by an amazing (if slightly dysfunctional) family that fully embraced the unwritten rules of French parenting. I was properly dressed, which is to say my mother dressed me, until I turned eighteen—unless, of course, we were at the beach, in which case I was naked until . . . let's just say *late*, later in life than anyone outside of Europe seems comfortable with. There were no choices, no explanations.

I had intended to raise my children in the same traditional fashion so that they, too, would know how to dress, how to eat, how to act. And then we moved to Brooklyn six years ago and I was introduced to a whole new way of parenting.

We were heading to drop the kids at school for the very first time, me wearing my Parisian uniform—little black dress, hat, and Louboutins—and my husband in his beret, literally with a baguette (a welcome gift from our new and very friendly neighbor) under his arm. My children were dressed head to toe in Bonpoint, *bien sûr*. We looked like aliens in a sea of printed leggings, colorful T-shirts, sneakers (some of them with flashing lights), and, to my great horror, TUTUS. In the afternoon at pick up, I noticed that no one was smoking in the school playground and that the American after-school snack had nothing to do with the French *goûter*.

That evening, while roasting a chicken for dinner and having a third glass of wine, I decided to try to adapt our family, at least a little. It seemed impossible at first— none of us even owned sneakers at that time—but before I realized it I was asking my children to wear helmets when they rode their bicycles and explaining to my little one, who is six, why it is not okay to paint her nails—even though I know the French thing to do would be just to say no decisively and leave it at that.

Which style is best? I still hold firm to many of my traditional ways, but I can tell you that the best approach is probably somewhere in the middle, a subtle mix of French authority and American enthusiasm. Our kids are very chic indeed, but yours look much happier.

—FLORENCE

I was raised by a loving family. My father, an artist, was obsessed with the beauty of things—though his opinion of beauty was admittedly sometimes a bit narrow, especially for a ten-year-old girl. I had to keep my hair short throughout my childhood—and even today my long hair remains a sensitive subject. I couldn't wear the shoes or clothes I wanted until I left for college. My parents raised me the classic French way, where children follow the rules and don't make them. I was constantly being told: *Don't talk with your mouth full. No elbows on the table. Stand up straight!* I don't blame them for a minute—especially because they also introduced me to American culture.

Though my grandmother was a Native American from the Huron tribe in Canada, I first visited North America at the age of twelve; my mom sent me to live with a family in Connecticut for the summer to learn English. There, I quickly discovered I could wear what I wanted, eat what I wanted, and go to bed when I wanted. I was free. After many more summers learning English, always with the same incredible family, it's not surprising that I chose to move to New York with my husband nine years ago. Both of my children were born here and attend American schools.

Far more shocking to my family in France is that I have broken French parenting rule number one, which pretty much dictates that children exist in the background of their parents' lives. My kids are the center of my universe. Even worse, I have the terrible habit of explaining things to my six-year-old son and valuing his opinion. I am relieved that I can finally proudly say out loud that there are toys scattered around our living room and I breastfed my babies. No French mother would ever admit to such things!

When Florence and I get together we always compare notes. While our parenting approaches are pretty different—she sticks more closely to the traditional French way we were raised, and I have embraced the American style with open arms—we always agree on one thing: if we were raising our kids together, they'd be perfect!

—Pauline

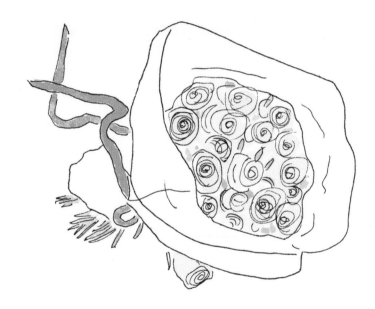

Greetings

From a young age, children are taught to say, "Bonjour, Madame" or "Bonjour, Monsieur" when they meet an adult, whether one of their parents' friends, the supermarket cashier, or the bus driver. A simple "hi" is considered rude.

Bonjour, Madame

Informal greetings abound.
Children feel comfortable calling adults
by their first name, without having
been invited to do so.

La bise

HUGS

As soon as they begin talking, French children must know how to choose between *tu* (the informal "you," for parents and friends) and the formal *vous** (for all other adults).

S'il vous plait, Madame...

**In certain very aristocratic families, children will even use* vous *with their parents for the rest of their lives.*

Everyone is equal:
kids, parents, grandparents,
teachers, animals, the president
of the United States.

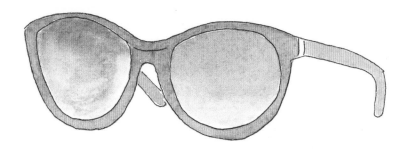

Style & Beauty

Parisian children wear
no more than three colors
at a time and very few
(always discreet) patterns.
Bright or loud colors are
to be avoided at all cost.
Leather shoes and an accessory or
two complete the look.
Children do not choose
their own outfits.

In New York, children
express their personality
and individuality when
getting dressed. Clothes are
comfortable and let them
move around, so there are lots
of leggings and sweatshirts.
There's no limit to the number
of colors and patterns in a
single outfit.

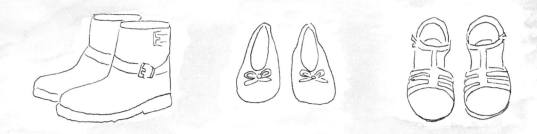

Sneakers are for sports only or, in a pinch, when riding a bike.*

*And, needless to say, white socks are worn only *with sneakers.*

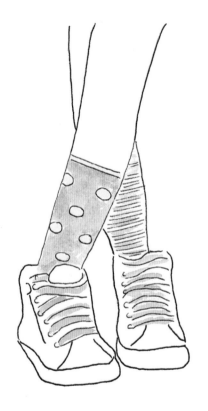

Sneakers go with everything.*

*So do white socks—or, even better, mismatched socks!

Culottes are worn under dresses.

People think it's very cute to see a
flash of *culotte* when a
little girl does a cartwheel.

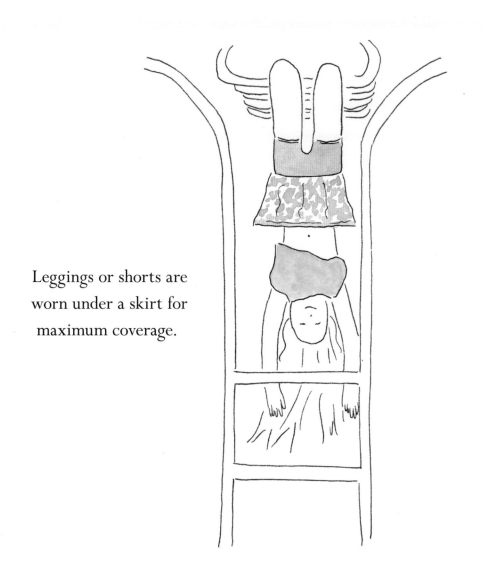

Leggings or shorts are worn under a skirt for maximum coverage.

No cartoon characters,
not even on underwear; solid colors
or perhaps sailor stripes are preferred.

Cartoon characters are **always** welcome, *especially* Disney ones.

No nail polish before age thirteen. In extremely
rare circumstances, clear polish is tolerated.

No heels before thirteen.
No exceptions.

The more nail colors (one per finger?) and decorations (flowers, hearts, rainbows), the better.

High-heeled sandals and princess shoes after age four.

Parisian haircuts for girls

Hairstyles in New York

Costumes, in public, are frowned upon. The one exception is
Mardi Gras—and even then it is preferable to put your child's
costume in her backpack so she can change at school.

I see you're a ballerina today!
Of course you can wear
your tutu to school.

Children wear costumes whenever and wherever
they want: to the park, a birthday party,
a restaurant, the supermarket, on an airplane ...

Hats, scarves, wicker baskets, and other adorable accessories
may annoy your children, but do not give in; they look adorable.
Style always comes first.

Style takes a backseat to the elements.

(It snows in New York.)

Meals

16h *le goûter*: A child may choose fruit, yogurt, or a chocolate croissant.

Anything goes for an afternoon snack: pizza, chips, ice cream, dried seaweed . . .

Go put your iPad in your room!

Sit up straight!

Don't put your elbows on the table!

Close your mouth while you chew!

Stay seated! Don't lick your knife!

Taste a bit of everything.

Don't serve yourself huge portions!

Don't play with your food.

Don't talk with your mouth full!

Put your napkin on your lap!

Hey sweetie, are you comfortable eating under the table?

Do you want a pillow maybe?

(She's such a character, isn't she?!)

20h

Dinner as a family. Children may not start their meal
before everyone is at the table and has been served.

6:00 p.m. onward

Families often eat in shifts, after soccer practice,
violin lessons, math tutoring …

Legs under the table, feet on the floor.

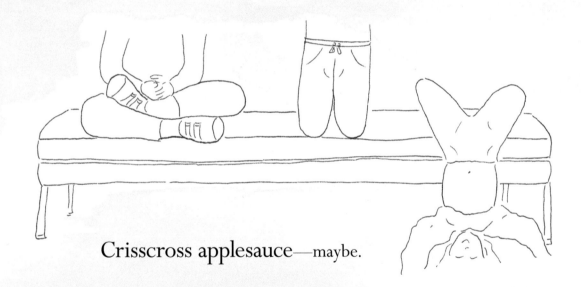

Crisscross applesauce—maybe.

Yippee!
Roast chicken with potato-and-leek gratin!

Ugh.

Can I have macaroni and cheese instead?

Don't eat with your hands!*

You're not a baby.

*Exceptions: bread, asparagus, and artichokes

Go ahead and eat with your hands—
whatever is easiest for you.

You can cry all you want,
but you aren't leaving the
table until you finish
your green beans.

If you don't like it,
you don't have to eat it.

Above all,
don't force yourself.

School

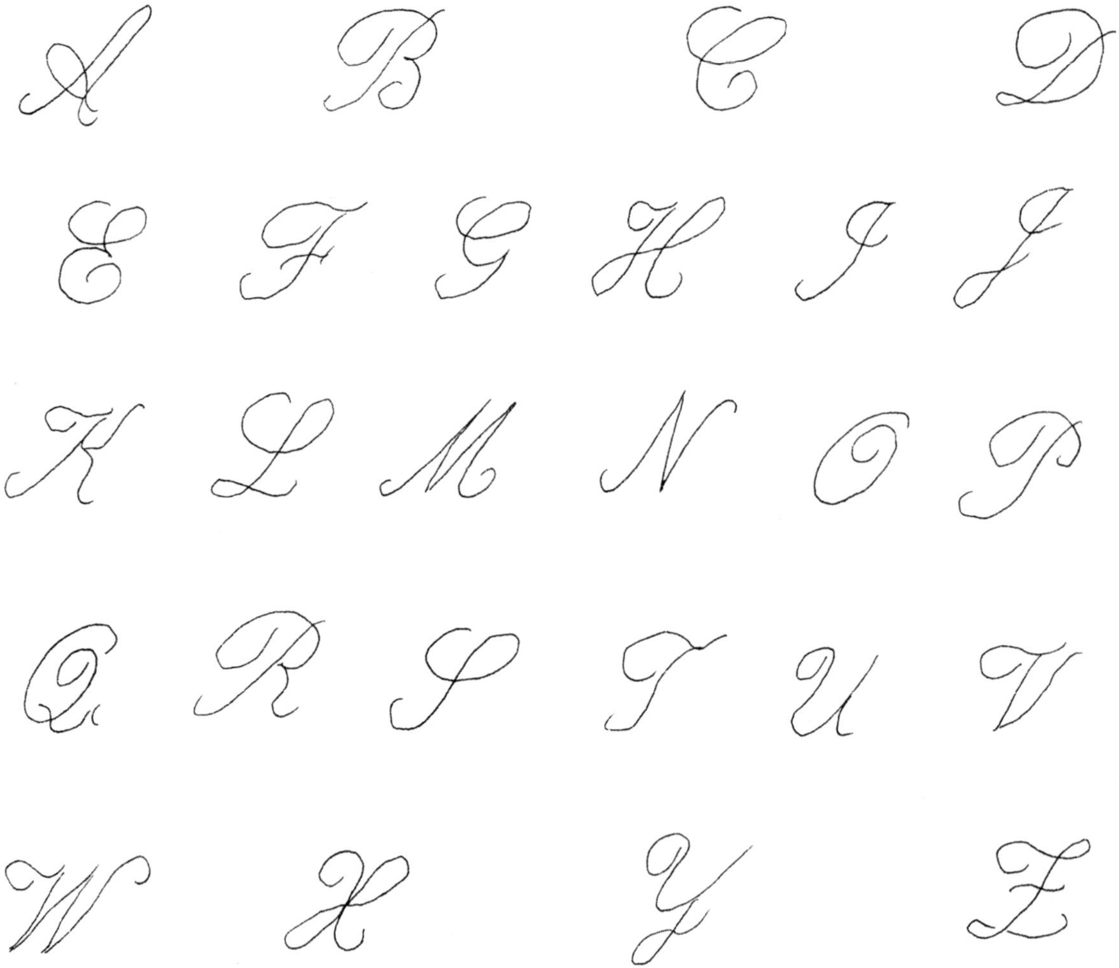

A B C D

E F G H I J

K L M N O P

Q R S T U V

W X Y Z

In Paris, school is for learning. It is not a fun place, and children don't like to go. "You can do better" is a French teacher's favorite phrase.

In New York, students learn by playing and participating in class, whether they like it or not. Children must be comfortable sharing opinions at a young age.

Pas mal*

*NOT BAD

OMG!!! YOU ARE SO **AWESOME!**
THAT IS GREAT,
YOU ARE A GENIUS !!
GOOD JOB.
EXCELLENT. YOU ARE SO
CREATIVE
AND SMART!!!
THAT IS INCREDIBLE !
HIGH FIVE !!!

French school cafeteria lunch tray

American lunch box

You got an A- in math.
Not bad, but next time try to get an A.

You got a C, but you did your best.
Good job!

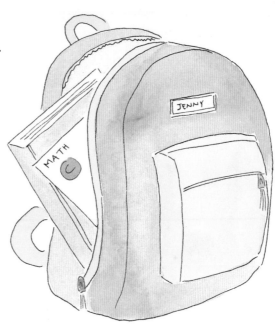

Baby Years

A baby shower in Paris

A baby shower in New York

The Parisian baby sits in his playpen.

Silently.

Music, gymnastics, yoga, swimming . . .

In New York, babies are booked solid; they LOVE activities.

Oh là là !

You're

still

breast feeding ?!

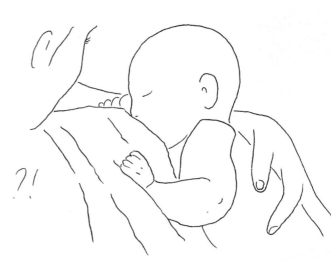

OMG! You're

NOT

breastfeeding

?!

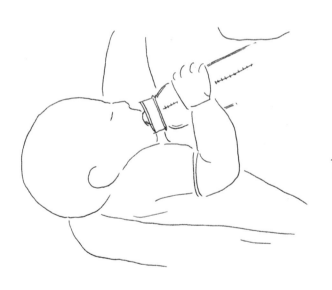

Diapers are gone by age two,
no matter what.

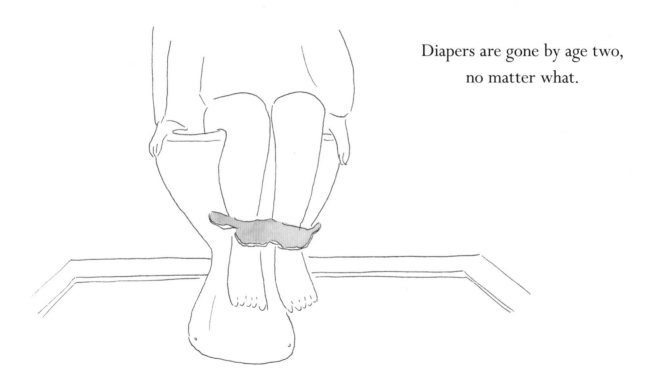

(Parents want to make sure that their child will be ready for school.)

Parents wait until
their child is READY.

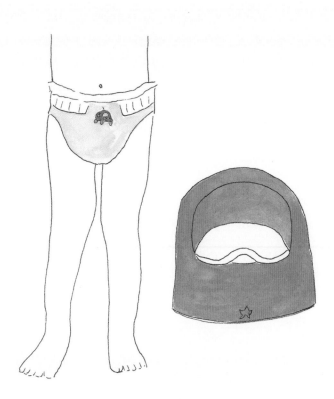

(It's not like he's going to go to college in diapers, right?)

Mothers let babies cry for a bit before comforting them.

They are already teaching them the golden rule:
not to interrupt the adults.

American mothers pick up their babies as soon as they make a peep.

Mommy time in Paris

Mommy time in New York

Playtime

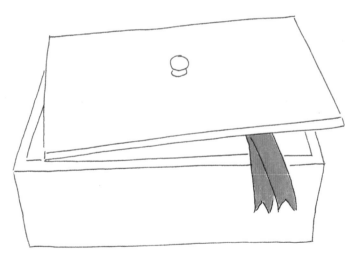

One time I won a tennis match.
My parents put the ribbon in a
box in my room.

I get a trophy every time
I participate. Everyone gets one,
even if you lose. They all go on
the mantel in the living room!

Well then, darling,
use your imagination.

Let's play together!
Do you want to play chess? Wii?
Soccer, baseball? We can draw or
do a puzzle? Play Monopoly?
Do you want a snack?

You can easily recognize French children
at the playground because they wear
leather shoes and nobody is helping them
at the monkey bars.

You'll probably find the mother sitting on a bench some
distance away, smoking a cigarette.

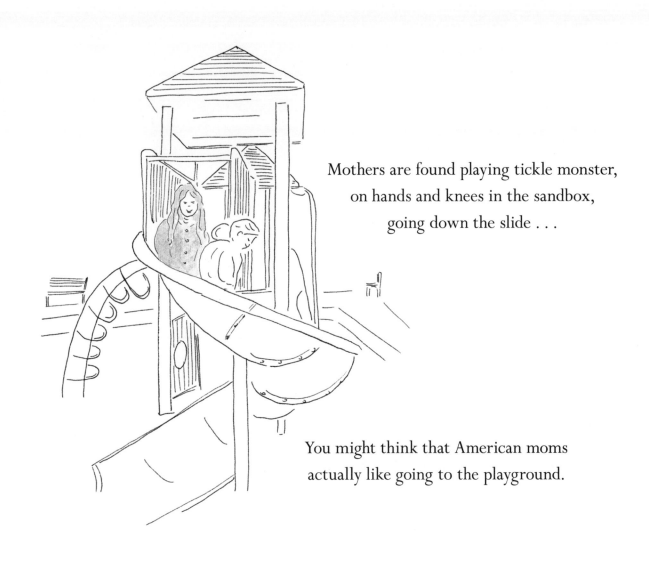

Mothers are found playing tickle monster,
on hands and knees in the sandbox,
going down the slide . . .

You might think that American moms
actually like going to the playground.

Playdates are rare in Paris. If, by chance,
you invite over a friend who has a child the same
age as yours, the children will be encouraged to play together
in the other room without making too much noise while the mothers chat.

Playdates are an institution. Parents
(usually moms) or nannies follow the kids from
room to room, taking part in the games.

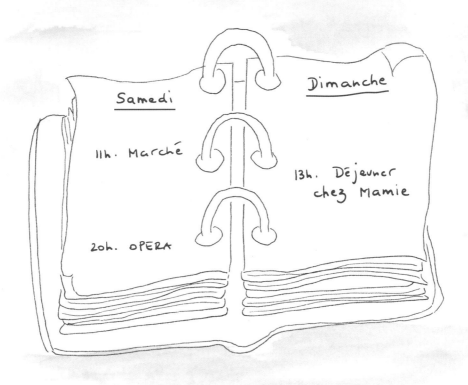

On the weekend, children follow the adults' schedules.

SATURDAY

8am	Soccer Practice
11am	museum of natural history
~~1pm~~	~~BARBECUE~~ : Cancelled
4pm	Birthday Party!
	Sleepover at Jake's house

SUNDAY

9am	Pick up from Jake's house
10am	Picnic in Central Park
12pm	BIRTHDAY PARTY
2pm	Block party
4:30pm	Movie and Dinner with SARA

On weekends, we do lots of activities!

Parisian parents do not stay and watch their child during sports practice.

They leave and come back at the end of the hour.
They have better things to do.

Parents encourage and **cheer** for
their children—

and for Emma, Max, Sofia, Mason, Olivia, Louis, and Clea, too.

Parisian parents do not interfere in playground disagreements.

Children have to learn how to resolve problems by themselves.

Parents are very involved in
playground drama
to make sure everyone
is sharing and no one's
feelings are getting hurt.

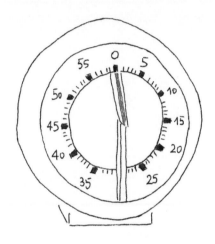

Discipline

I said no.

No means no.

*Listen, my love, I know you want to go to
school in your swimsuit today but it is snowing
outside so you are going to feel very, very cold and I
don't want you to get sick because then we would have
to go to the doctor and maybe to the hospital. . . . What
if you put your swimsuit under your clothes so that you
feel like you are wearing it anyway? What do you think
about that? I understand you are very frustrated and I
don't want you to have a bad day, so let's try
to solve this situation together.*

*Can't you see
I am
talking?*

French children must never interrupt an
adult conversation under any circumstance.

American mothers are always willing to listen.

You hit your sister with
your Harry Potter wand?
No TV for one month!

Tell me why you hit your sister
with your Harry Potter wand.
Do you want to talk about it?
Were you jealous?
Did you feel as if she were
stealing our affection?

French children live in their **parents'** home.

American parents live in their **children's** home.

Go to your room
until dinnertime!

*Time out. I'll come
back in five minutes so
we can talk about
what happened.*

Vacation

À la plage

AT THE BEACH

Long family vacation

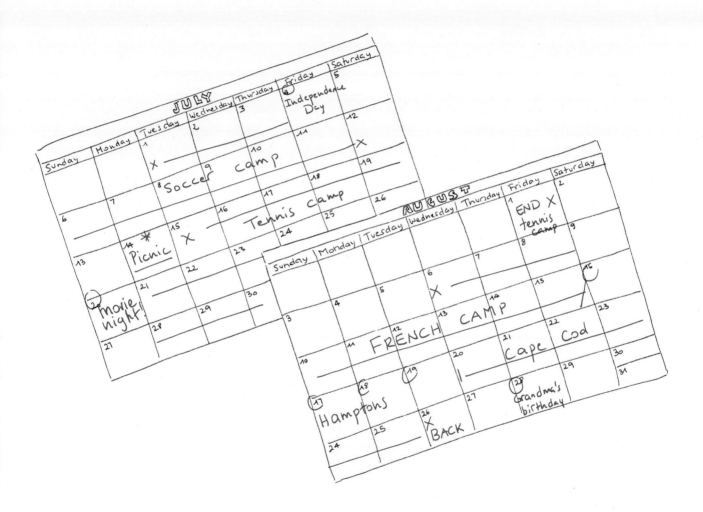

Long summer camp, short family vacation

On y va, les enfants. *We can skip the line.*

I know you're tired, sweetie, but we have to wait our turn just like everyone else.

Parties & Holidays

Mothers might invite a few very close friends over to the house and bake a chocolate cake at most for a child's birthday.

The children play for up to two hours and eat candy.

Juggler, clown, magician, balloon artist, face painter, rock climbing—
constant entertainment is expected at a birthday party, along with pizza and
cupcakes and, of course, a goodie bag for everyone.

The whole class is invited with their siblings,
plus camp friends, and also the soccer team.

She opens her gifts in front of her friends

and says thank you for each,
even if she is disappointed.

He opens presents after the party.

Thank-you cards follow weeks later,
if the parents can manage to figure out who gave him
which gift—and find everyone's mailing address.

Halloween?

What's that?

Trick or treat!

Elaborate costumes are decided
weeks in advance.

HAPPY HOLIDAYS!

Around Town

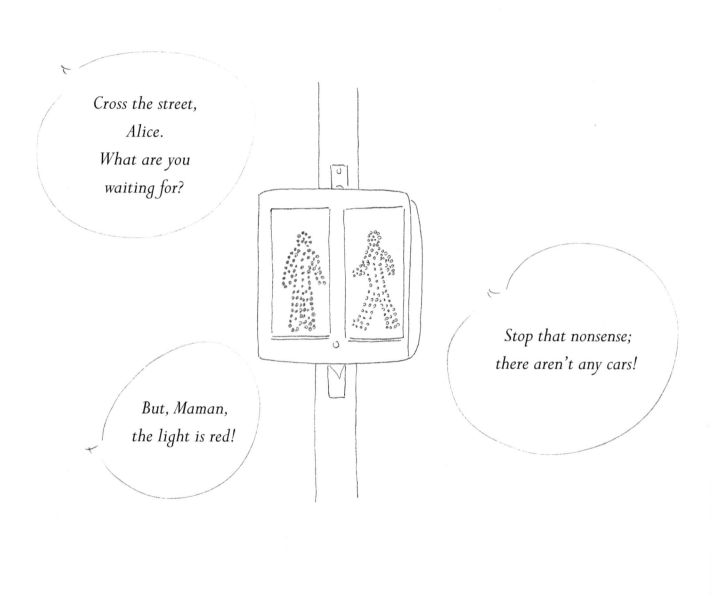

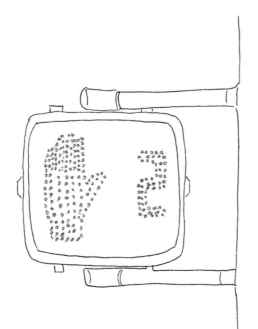

Watch out, darling,
the light is red and we
have to wait until we get
the signal to cross.

Stop smiling like that; you look like an idiot.

Look how **happy** *she is!*

Please lower your voice, sweetheart.
You're giving me a headache.

Yes, darling,
I love carousels, too!

Just go behind that tree.

Good, that means you'll enjoy
your dinner tonight.

My poor darling!
Do you want some Goldfish,
Pirate's Booty, cheese sticks?
Maybe a juice box?

Health

Close the window.
You will catch a cold!

Open the window.
Let's get some fresh air!

No dentist visits
before age six.

Dentist at age two.
Flossing is an obsession.

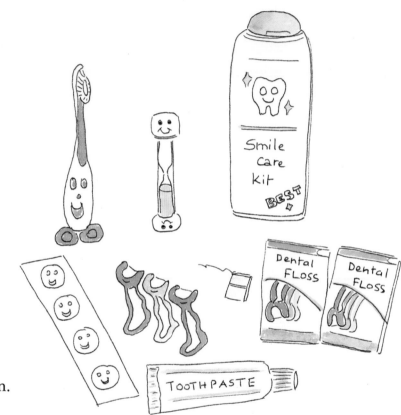

You don't need a helmet; it's not like you're
made of glass. Besides, the helmet
makes you look ridiculous!

Put your helmet on, sweetie! It's very dangerous—you could fall and hurt yourself!

Stop crying!
You're not even bleeding!

Oh no, my poor baby!
You got a boo-boo?
Let me put Neosporin on it.
Do you want a Hello Kitty
Band-Aid?

*You have to watch
your figure, Josephine.
You've had too much
chocolate already!*

*Would you like **another** piece of chocolate, Josie?*

ACKNOWLEDGMENTS

My husband and my children
My parents and my sister, Virginie

FM

My husband and my children
My parents
Leo and Louis

PL

Rica Allannic
Stephanie Huntwork
Debbie Glasserman
Cathy Hennessy
Linnea Knollmueller
Susanna Lea
Julia Wagner

FM & PL

ABOUT THE AUTHORS

FLORENCE MARS is the vice president of Bonpoint in the United States. Prior to joining the company, she worked for Louis Vuitton and L'Oréal and as a producer for Elephant and RadicalMedia. She is on the board of the Epic Foundation and also the Baan Dek Foundation, which helps migrant kids in Chiang Mai, Thailand. Mars lives in Brooklyn with her husband and their three children.

PAULINE LÉVÊQUE is a French journalist turned illustrator. She wrote about the film and entertainment industries for publications including *Le Journal du Dimanche* and *Paris Match,* where she was a contributor for ten years. When her son was born, she wrote and illustrated *Beep Beep,* a bilingual (French-English) children's book series starring a funny little red car. Lévêque has written four books and is currently working on Beep Beep's newest adventure. She lives in Manhattan with her husband, a well-known French author, and their two children.